Air Force Service Procurement

Approaches for Measurement and Management

Laura H. Baldwin, John A. Ausink, Nancy Nicosia

Prepared for the United States Air Force

Approved for public release; distribution unlimited

PROJECT AIR FORCE

The research reported here was sponsored by the United States Air Force under contract F49642-01-C-0003. Further information may be obtained from the Strategic Planning Division, Directorate of Plans, Hq USAF.

Library of Congress Cataloging-in-Publication Data

Baldwin, Laura H., 1967–
    Air Force service procurement : approaches for measurement and management /
Laura H. Baldwin, John A. Ausink, Nancy Nicosia.
      p. cm.
    "MG-299."
    Includes bibliographical references.
    ISBN 0-8330-3714-5 (pbk. : alk. paper)
    I. Ausink, John A. II. Nicosia, Nancy. III. Title.

UC267.B35 2005
358.4'16212'0973—dc22

                                      2004028312

Published 2005 by the RAND Corporation
1776 Main Street, P.O. Box 2138, Santa Monica, CA 90407-2138
1200 South Hayes Street, Arlington, VA 22202-5050
201 North Craig Street, Suite 202, Pittsburgh, PA 15213-1516
RAND URL: http://www.rand.org/
To order RAND documents or to obtain additional information, contact
Distribution Services: Telephone: (310) 451-7002;
Fax: (310) 451-6915; Email: order@rand.org

Preface

This report documents RAND Corporation research on a portfolio of metrics that may be useful in managing service acquisitions for the Air Force Program Executive Officer for Combat and Mission Support (AFPEO/CM). This research is based on a series of interviews with commercial sector purchasing professionals who are respected by their peers for their successful creation and implementation of what are widely accepted as best purchasing and supply management practices, particularly in the area of service acquisitions.

This research was part of a broader study entitled "Supporting Air Force Procurement Transformation and Laying the Groundwork for Services Acquisition Reform," sponsored by the Air Force Deputy Assistant Secretary for Contracting and conducted within the Resource Management Program of RAND Project AIR FORCE.

This report is designed to assist federal agency personnel seeking to identify opportunities for improving the outcomes of purchased goods and services through application of best practices for purchasing and supply management. As such, it assumes a basic understanding of best commercial purchasing and supply management practices. Readers may also be interested in the following related RAND documents (which are available on the web, see http://www.rand.org/Abstracts):

- *Air Force Procurement Workforce Transformation: Lessons from the Commercial Sector,* John Ausink, Laura H. Baldwin, and Christopher Paul, MG-214-AF, 2004.

- *Defining Needs and Managing Performance of Installation Support Contracts: Perspectives from the Commercial Sector,* Laura H. Baldwin and Sarah Hunter, MR-1812-AF, 2004.
- *Measuring Changes in Service Costs to Meet the Requirements of the 2002 National Defense Authorization Act,* Chad Shirley, John Ausink, and Laura H. Baldwin, MR-1821-AF, 2004.
- *Using a Spend Analysis to Help Identify Prospective Air Force Purchasing and Supply Management Initiatives: Summary of Selected Findings,* Nancy Y. Moore, Cynthia R. Cook, Charles Lindenblatt, and Clifford A. Grammich, DB-434-AF, 2004.
- *Implementing Best Purchasing and Supply Management Practices: Lessons from Innovative Commercial Firms,* Nancy Y. Moore, Laura H. Baldwin, Frank Camm, and Cynthia R. Cook, DB-334-AF, 2002.
- *Implementing Performance-Based Services Acquisition (PBSA): Perspectives from an Air Logistics Center and a Product Center,* John Ausink, Laura H. Baldwin, Sarah Hunter, and Chad Shirley, DB-388-AF, 2002.
- *Federal Contract Bundling: A Framework for Making and Justifying Decisions for Purchased Services,* Laura H. Baldwin, Frank Camm, and Nancy Y. Moore, MR-1224-AF, 2001.
- *Performance-Based Contracting in the Air Force: A Report on Experiences in the Field,* John Ausink, Frank Camm, and Charles Cannon, DB-342-AF, 2001.
- *Strategic Sourcing: Measuring and Managing Performance,* Laura H. Baldwin, Frank Camm, and Nancy Y. Moore, DB-287-AF, 2000.
- *Incentives to Undertake Sourcing Studies in the Air Force,* Laura H. Baldwin, Frank Camm, Edward G. Keating, and Ellen M. Pint, DB-240-AF, 1998.
- *Strategic Sourcing: Theory and Evidence from Economics and Business Management,* Ellen M. Pint and Laura H. Baldwin, MR-865-AF, 1997.

RAND Project AIR FORCE

RAND Project AIR FORCE (PAF), a division of the RAND Corporation, is the U.S. Air Force's federally funded research and development center for studies and analyses. PAF provides the Air Force with independent analyses of policy alternatives affecting the development, employment, combat readiness, and support of current and future aerospace forces. Research is conducted in four programs: Aerospace Force Development; Manpower, Personnel, and Training; Resource Management; and Strategy and Doctrine.

Additional information about PAF is available on our web site at http://www.rand.org/paf.

Contents

Figure and Tables

Figure

Tables

Summary

To satisfy requirements in the fiscal year 2002 National Defense Authorization Act (U.S. Congress, 2001) to improve the acquisition of services by the Department of Defense, the Air Force established a Program Executive Officer for Combat and Mission Support (AFPEO/CM) who is responsible for management and oversight of a well-defined portfolio of Air Force services acquisition activities. This office is the single point of contact for Air Force services acquisition inquiries and is also responsible for developing long-range plans for cost-effective acquisition of services.

To fulfill its responsibilities, the AFPEO/CM needs metrics to help it monitor compliance with statutory requirements, needs to respond to congressional inquiries about specific acquisitions, and needs to effectively manage Air Force services acquisition activities and organizations. RAND Project AIR FORCE was asked to help develop a portfolio of "overarching" measures that will allow the AFPEO/CM to assess the health of Air Force acquisition activities, diagnose problems, and target improvement efforts. This report describes our recommendations.

To help develop this portfolio of metrics, we considered the experience of commercial firms, which have long had a "strategic" view of purchasing direct materials (goods) because they are direct inputs to production, but have only recently explored applying such approaches to purchasing services. Through interviews with well-respected chief purchasing officers and other executives involved in service acquisitions, through conference participation, and through a review of the business literature, we found that commercial firms are beginning to manage their service acquisitions in a manner similar to their acquisition of direct materials. That is, commercial firms are increasingly making use of commodity councils (cross-functional teams) to develop purchasing and supply management strategies for services and are developing and using performance metrics, similar to those used for goods, to manage their purchased services and their purchasing organizations (pp. 11–12).

Purchasing and Supply Management Strategies

Ideally, corporate objectives flow down through the purchasing organization and are supported through formal strategies for individual commodity groups, as well as personnel incentives. Strategies are based on intensive market research and assessments of internal demands for services. Because of the many facets of purchasing and supply management strategies, commodity councils typically include a variety of experts such as representatives of user groups, experts in purchasing/acquisition, and experts in the particular service industry. Industry experts or other stakeholders, rather than procurement personnel, may be tapped to lead commodity councils (pp. 11–17).

Commercial Approaches to Metrics

Commercial firms rely on results-oriented metrics that focus on how acquisition activities support corporate objectives to manage their service acquisition activities. The categories of results-oriented metrics that appeared most often in our research include cost, quality, supplier satisfaction, implementation of new initiatives, and special interest items. In addition to these results-oriented metrics, commercial firms indicated that management metrics that track internal customer satisfaction, personnel training and retention, and ethics violations are also important. Selected metrics are reported to top-level executives on a regular basis (pp. 19–35).

Developing a baseline for these metrics and then tracking them over time present challenges for many firms. Some firms have adopted new management information systems to collect and organize the data for their service acquisitions and have implemented surveys to collect additional data such as supplier satisfaction and customer satisfaction with purchased services, the purchasing organization, and its processes (p. 34).

Recommendations for the Air Force

While not a commercial firm, the Air Force can learn from commercial firms' experiences in managing its service acquisitions. We recommend a balanced portfolio of performance metrics for the AFPEO/CM based on the six major categories of metrics discussed above (pp. 37–50). These metrics are listed in Table S.1.

As with commercial firms, populating these metrics will be challenging for the Air Force. Some of the required data, such as contract costs, exist in Air Force contracting data systems. However, we have concerns about the integrity of these data and their usefulness in determining what services the Air Force purchases (Dixon et al., forthcoming). The Air Force will need to implement new data collection procedures for many of the required data, particularly supplier and customer satisfaction data (pp. 38–50).

Because of commercial sector successes and limited federal government experience with centralized purchasing strategies, we recommend the Air Force adopt a centralized, strategic approach linked to Air Force objectives for managing its purchased services. Proposed Department of Defense–wide commodity councils for selected categories of services are a step in this direction. Given the diversity of service users and their requirements, it will be important to include all-important user groups in the process of developing strategies for categories of services. Other key stakeholders such as small business advocates should be included in the process as well. The Air Force will need to reinforce these efforts with leadership support and incentives that are aligned with Air Force objectives (pp. 50–54).

Table S.1
Proposed Portfolio of Metrics for the AFPEO/CM

Metrics Category	Potential Metrics
Cost	Change in costs versus change in market index
	Actual versus projected post-study costs for recently completed A-76 studies
	Procurement return on investment
Quality	Customer satisfaction with purchased services
	Reliability or continuity of services
Supplier satisfaction	Supplier satisfaction with doing business with the Air Force
New initiatives	Process and outcome metrics for specific initiatives, which may include • purchasing and supply management • management and oversight of acquisition of services process • customer education
Special interest	Compliance • Percentage of service dollars and contracts awarded to different categories of small businesses • Percentage of service contracts that are performance based
	Other • Percentage of A-76 studies or slots that were successfully competed within the required time frame • Number of protests resulting from A-76 awards • Percentage of key staff for A-76 studies that remain in their jobs throughout those studies • Percentage of provider personnel that remain in their jobs for a given period of time
Internal management	Internal customer satisfaction with the Air Force purchasing process and personnel
	Percentage of dollars associated with purchases executed outside the Air Force's preferred strategy (i.e., maverick buying)

Acknowledgments

We wish to thank the purchasing professionals who took time to meet with us and teach us about their approaches to managing their firms' service acquisitions. Assurances of anonymity prevent us from identifying them here, but this research would not have been possible without their help.

We thank Steve Busch, AFPEO/CM, for his help in shaping this research to ensure that it addressed the correct issues and concerns.

We are also grateful to our RAND colleagues Lloyd Dixon, Edward Keating, Nancy Moore, and Chad Shirley for their insights on Air Force service acquisitions and data. Nick Castle and Chris Nelson provided helpful comments on an early draft of this report. Judy Lesso, from the RAND library, helped conduct our literature review; Mary DeBold provided document preparation assistance; and Christina Pitcher's skillful editing added clarity to our final manuscript.

Abbreviations and Acronyms

AFPEO/CM	Air Force Program Executive Officer for Combat and Mission Support
CAPS	Center for Advanced Purchasing Studies
CPO	Chief Purchasing Officer
DoD	Department of Defense
FAR	Federal Acquisition Regulations
GAO	General Accounting Office
ISM	Institute for Supply Management
MEO	Most Efficient Organization
NIB/NISH	National Industries for the Blind/National Industries for the Severely Handicapped
PBSA	Performance-Based Services Acquisition
PEO	Program Executive Officer
ROI	Return on Investment

CHAPTER ONE

Introduction

Federal agencies purchase a wide range of goods and services each year. During the 1990s, services became an increasingly important spending category, and they currently represent the largest category of government purchases. The Department of Defense (DoD) is the largest purchaser of services within the federal government, spending approximately $93 billion on services in fiscal year 2002 (FY02). This represents an increase of 18 percent since FY01.[1] Services purchased by the DoD include commercial services for installations and facilities such as building maintenance, grounds keeping, and janitorial services; professional services such as consulting and engineering support; and weapon system services such as research and development, test and evaluation, and maintenance and modification activities.

The DoD has long sought to ensure that its appropriations are used as effectively and efficiently as possible. When acquisition reform—which encompasses a wide range of changes to procurement regulations, policies, and practices—received increasing emphasis during the 1990s, early efforts focused on the purchase of weapon systems and other hardware. However, as services have grown in budgetary importance, acquisition reform for service purchases has become a priority.[2]

---

[1] For more details, see GAO (2003), GAO (2002), GAO (2001), and Davis (2001).

[2] In principle, the same kinds of reforms should be applicable to both goods and services. As we will see in Chapters Two and Three, management philosophies and metrics used by commercial firms for categories of purchased goods and services are quite similar.

Traditional service contracts specified how providers should perform the work rather than allowing them the freedom to pursue the best way to meet their customers' needs. One tenet of services acquisition reform shifts federal agencies away from this paradigm toward the use of performance-based contracts. Part 37.601 of the Federal Acquisition Regulations (FAR) defines four requirements of a performance-based service contract: (1) tell the contractor what is needed, rather than how to provide the service; (2) establish measurable performance standards and a quality assurance plan to determine whether the service meets the contract requirements; (3) reduce the fee or price when the service does not meet those requirements (negative incentives); and (4) use performance (positive) incentives where appropriate. The combination of an outcome orientation and focus on incentives is meant to promote service innovation and reduce costs.

Performance-based service contracts gained attention in the federal government in the early 1990s (Office of Federal Procurement Policy, 1991).[3] The Air Force issued an instruction for implementing performance-based service contracts in 1999, which was updated in February 2004 (U.S. Air Force, 2004). In April 2000, Jacques Gansler, the Undersecretary of Defense for Acquisition and Technology, established a goal that a minimum of 50 percent of DoD service acquisitions, measured in both dollars and contracts, be performance based by the year 2005 (Gansler, 2000). The Office of Management and Budget affirmed the use of performance-based contracts across the federal government in a March 2001 memorandum by establishing an interim goal that 20 percent of FY02 federal service contract dollars be awarded through performance-based contracts (O'Keefe, 2001). In addition, the National Defense Authorization Act for FY02 (U.S. Congress, 2001) (hereafter referred to as the FY02 Act) prohib-

---

[3] See Diernisse (2003) for another discussion of the evolution of performance-based service contracts.

ited the use of service contracts in the DoD that are not performance based without prior approval.[4]

To encourage the DoD to fundamentally change the way it approaches its services acquisition activities, the FY02 Act included a requirement to demonstrate 10 percent savings in service contract costs (relative to a baseline of FY00 costs) by FY11 through use of performance-based service contracts, increased competition, and management innovations. The DoD was ordered to report estimates of savings to Congress annually through 2005.[5]

The FY02 Act also directed all DoD agencies to establish a management structure for the procurement of services that would be comparable to the structure used for the procurement of products. Each agency was to designate an official to be responsible for the management of the procurement of services. The Secretary of Defense was authorized by the FY02 Act to establish the dollar thresholds and other criteria for the approval of purchases of services, and agencies were required to collect and analyze data on purchases.

The FY03 version of the National Defense Authorization Act (U.S. Congress, 2002b) removed the specific savings goals of the FY02 Act, but assumed that savings would be achieved: Congress established the goal of using Performance-Based Service Acquisitions (PBSA) for 70 percent of all service acquisitions by 2011,[6] and it reduced the FY03 authorization for the purchase of services by $183 million.[7] The FY04 version of the National Defense Authorization Act further reinforces the preference for performance-based service contracts by amending the Office of Federal Procurement Policy Act so that performance-based contracts that satisfy certain conditions

---

[4] However, the definition of "performance based" in the act is different than the one in FAR Part 37. The act specifies that a performance-based contract "includes the use of performance work statements that set forth contract requirements in clear, specific, and objective terms with measurable outcomes." See U.S. Congress, 2001, Section 801.2330a.

[5] See U.S. Congress, 2001, Section 802, "Savings Goals for Procurements of Services."

[6] U.S. Congress, 2002b.

[7] U.S. Congress, 2002a, p. 683. This is approximately a 1.2 percent reduction, based on an assumed baseline of $50 billion in DoD service contracts.

may be treated as contracts for the procurement of commercial services (U.S. Congress, 2003, Subtitle C, Section 1431).

> [This] will give government customers more discretion to use best value as a determining factor over cost. The legislation allows government agencies greater flexibility in contracting for a variety of services available in the private sector, including sophisticated services such as management consulting (Phinney, 2003).

AFPEO/CM Office and Responsibilities

In accordance with the FY02 Act, the Air Force established a Program Executive Officer for Combat and Mission Support (AFPEO/CM), whose office is responsible for management and oversight of the Air Force's service acquisition activities that fall within the AFPEO/CM portfolio. This portfolio includes most service acquisitions greater than $100 million, public-private competitions conducted under the rules of the Office of Management and Budget Circular A-76 that involve 300 or more full-time equivalent positions, special interest service acquisitions, and other acquisitions that involve significant services. Exceptions include service acquisitions associated with weapon systems—these fall within the portfolio of the weapon system PEO—and federally funded research and development centers. Numbered Air Force services, construction, architect and engineering, and housing and utilities privatization activities are excluded from the AFPEO/CM's consideration as well.[8] As of November 2002, the AFPEO/CM's portfolio included over 120 service acquisition programs valued at over $60 billion.[9]

Among the many challenges the office faces are the identification of service acquisitions and the implementation of new strategies

---

[8] See interim changes to the Air Force Federal Acquisition Regulation Supplement Subpart 5337.5 (Clay, 2003) and Cardenas (2004).

[9] Per our discussion with Steve Busch, a support contractor in the AFPEO/CM office.

and initiatives.[10] One particular area of emphasis is implementation of performance-based contracts for services. The AFPEO/CM office determines whether service contracts are performance based and must approve the use of any contracts that are not performance based.

Early efforts of the AFPEO/CM office have focused on improving the execution of service acquisitions by developing and implementing the Management and Oversight of Acquisition of Services Process. This process implements the FY02 Act by establishing management controls and reviews to ensure the successful acquisition of services and the implementation of PBSA practices (Cardenas, 2004). Over time, the AFPEO/CM organization is expected to take on more strategic roles as well. As the single point of contact for Air Force service acquisition inquiries within the Air Force and the DoD, it will be responsible for developing long-range plans to ensure the effective and efficient acquisition of services. It will also be a key stakeholder in designing and implementing future purchasing and supply management strategies for Air Force services.

AFPEO/CM Metrics

Successful fulfillment of the AFPEO/CM's day-to-day responsibilities requires metrics that monitor compliance with statutory requirements (implementation of PBSA, achievement of savings goals, etc.), help respond to inquiries about specific acquisitions or contracts, and assist in the effective management of the organization (ensuring maintenance of certain skills for the workforce, for example). Metrics will also be required to ensure the effective management of service acquisitions and extract the most value from suppliers so that the Air Force can be a good steward of its resources. RAND Project AIR FORCE was asked to assist in the development of a portfolio of "overarching"

---

[10] This is not an easy problem. There is a great deal of disagreement in the Air Force about what should be considered a "service" (Ausink et al., 2002). In addition, some services fall under the domain of other PEOs; yet, they are still subject to Air Force policy on service acquisitions.

measures that would allow the PEO for services to assess the health of the Air Force's acquisition activities, diagnose problems, and target improvement efforts. Metrics in this portfolio were to be consistent with the metrics developed by RAND for the Air Force's Deputy Assistant Secretary for Contracting as part of the effort to transform the procurement workforce for the 21st century (see Ausink, Baldwin, and Paul, 2004). In developing this portfolio for the AFPEO/CM, RAND was asked to note particular challenges that the Air Force may have in implementing the recommended metrics.

Research Approach

The research described in this report is based on three different sources of information on well-respected commercial practices for managing services expenditures.

The primary source is a set of interviews with private sector experts whose duties paralleled some of those required of the AFPEO/CM. Project resources allowed us to interview five executives. Three of these individuals were chief purchasing officers (CPOs) in their organizations, one was a CPO's associate director, and one was a director of services with prior purchasing experience. These experts represented four different firms at the time of our interview,[11] but they had combined career experience across nine firms. Thus, in their responses, they drew from their experiences in implementing new purchasing practices multiple times in different organizations. We chose the four CPO interviewees based on their professional standing within their fields, determined by their association with professional organizations such as the Institute for Supply Management (ISM), their participation as invited speakers at professional conferences, and the professional literature. The director of services was chosen because of his extensive experience in both purchasing and services.

---

[11] We interviewed both the CPO and the associate director at one firm. We tried to set up an interview with the CPO from a fifth firm, but he declined because of his busy schedule.

Each interview was conducted during a two-to-three hour session.[12] The discussions were semi-structured, guided by a list of questions that were provided in advance to the interviewees. The Appendix contains the list of questions used in our interviews.

We also attended two purchasing-related conferences. At a conference on purchasing services sponsored by ISM,[13] we had an opportunity to meet with other purchasing professionals who were seeking ways to improve their acquisition processes as well as ways to measure their success in implementing new approaches. During a roundtable discussion for procurement executives sponsored by the SAS Institute,[14] we participated in discussions moderated by industry experts on topics such as supply base consolidation, procurement management, and managing organizational change.

Finally, we conducted an extensive review of the business literature, including journals and trade publications, to learn more about commercial practices in measuring and managing performance when procuring services.[15] One well-respected resource for such research is the Center for Advanced Purchasing Studies (CAPS).[16]

Project resources did not allow us to independently verify information provided in interviews, in conference presentations, or in the literature. However, we analyzed information from all three sources to seek insights and lessons that were consistent across sources. In the discussion of our findings, we provide specific examples to illustrate points and note areas in which practices differed across sources.

---

[12] Two interviews were conducted in person and involved three executives. The other two executives were interviewed over the phone.

[13] "Smart Business: Leveraging the Services Spend," December 5–6, 2002, Scottsdale, Arizona.

[14] Procurement Executive Roundtable, June 5, 2003, Ritz-Carlton Hotel, Arlington, Virginia.

[15] We used a variety of search terms for the business literature review, including purchased services, service contracts, services and purchasing, and metrics and services. Judy Lesso, from the RAND library, conducted the literature search for us.

[16] More information about CAPS can be found at www.capsresearch.org.

The services discussed in our research sources are similar to the commercial-like services purchased by the Air Force. These include facilities services (building maintenance, custodial services, security services, and landscaping), telecommunications (information technology services, computing, help desks, and call centers), and various other support services (human resources, temporary help, consulting, outplacement, food services, and day care). However, the AFPEO/CM is also responsible for some services that are more complicated than those usually found in the commercial world, such as comprehensive testing services for complex weapon systems.

Preview of Findings

Our primary finding is that well-respected purchasing professionals are beginning to manage their service expenditures in the same way that they manage their goods expenditures. Our more detailed research findings can be divided into two categories: those related to management practices and those related to the implementation of performance metrics.

We found that expenditures for services are a relatively new area of focus for commercial firms implementing strategic purchasing and supply management practices. Firms are expanding their development of corporate-wide purchasing strategies tied to organizational objectives beyond the purchase of goods, to include categories of services as well. Commercial successes with this approach suggest that the Air Force could benefit from leveraging expenditures for commonly purchased services across the Air Force, DoD, or even other agencies.

In addition, commercial firms track services procurement using metrics similar to those that they use for goods procurement. Most metrics focus on procurement outcomes. The five most frequently mentioned outcome categories were cost, quality, supplier satisfaction, metrics for new initiatives (such as supplier development), and special interest metrics (such as measures of small business participation). Other metrics, such as personnel retention levels, are used to track internal organizational management. Commercial firms are careful to ensure that metrics reinforce and measure progress toward achieving both short-term and long-term corporate objectives.

Organization of the Report

The remainder of this report is organized as follows. Chapter Two discusses the management issues associated with service procurement in the commercial world, including the formulation of purchasing strategies, the use and composition of commodity councils (cross-functional teams), and the use of performance incentives. Chapter Three describes how commercial firms use metrics to monitor progress in achieving corporate goals, including types of metrics used, data collection, and how results are reported. Chapter Four discusses our recommendations for how the Air Force can adopt and adapt relevant management lessons and metrics from the commercial sector. This chapter highlights the use of a balanced portfolio of metrics to monitor the health of Air Force acquisition, potential difficulties in data collection, and the implementation of commodity councils for services. The Appendix contains the questionnaires that we used to guide our interviews.

CHAPTER TWO

Commercial Strategies for Service Procurement

Increased spending on services is not unique to the federal government; commercial firms are also spending more in this area. CAPS Research noted in 2002 that services spending in the broader economy "represents a large and growing segment of organizations' overall purchases" (CAPS Research, 2002). A year later, CAPS reported that in a survey of firms with annual revenues ranging from less than $1 billion to over $60 billion, firms on average expected their spending on services to increase 13 percent over the next five years, with more than half of the firms in the survey expecting their spending on services to increase on average by 22 percent. Overall services spending for these firms represented 31 percent of the total spending on purchases, and 11 percent of total revenue (CAPS Research, 2003).[1]

Because direct materials, or "goods," are direct inputs to production and were in the past more significant drivers of expenditures, commercial firms have long viewed them as obvious candidates for "strategic" management. That is, firms have recognized the importance of purchasing and supply management approaches—such as developing closer relationships with key suppliers and undertaking supplier development efforts—that improve the likelihood of achieving the long-term goals of the corporation. In contrast, our interviews indicate that there has been much less emphasis on applying similar approaches to service acquisitions. Responsibility for pur-

---

[1] This is consistent with a recent Aberdeen Group survey of 77 business and supply chain executives. On average, services represented 34 percent of total purchases for survey respondents' organizations (Aberdeen Group, 2003).

chasing services has traditionally been delegated to lower levels in an organization, with little—if any—coordination among the end users. In a series of focus group discussions with purchasing professionals, Smeltzer and Ogden (2002) found that top management generally has viewed service acquisitions as less complex than materials acquisitions and has excluded purchasing organizations from service purchases. As a result of the greater emphasis on materials purchases, there are fewer tools for purchasing and supply management activities for services than there are for materials. For example, cost analyses are reportedly more difficult for services because there are fewer models for the total cost of ownership and fewer formal training opportunities for service acquisition activities.

The current large levels of spending on services and the expected increases are now leading commercial firms to enlarge the role of purchasing organizations in the acquisition of services in order to extract greater value from them (Smeltzer and Ogden, 2002).[2] Two important dimensions of this approach that are discussed as best practices in the literature and implemented by the well-respected practitioners who were our interviewees are (1) the use of "commodity councils," which are centralized cross-functional teams, to develop and implement optimal purchasing and supply management strategies that are linked to corporate objectives for some categories of services and (2) the application of performance metrics. This chapter discusses the development of purchasing strategies.

---

[2] Avery (2003) shows that in a recent *Purchasing Magazine* survey of 1,000 buying operations in the United States, 77 percent of respondents said that purchasing organizations are becoming more involved in the process of buying services. The primary reported benefits are cost reductions, better quality services, and improved supplier relationships. The Aberdeen Group's survey indicated that 72 percent of respondents' companies are utilizing formal procedures for managing their service acquisitions, although their approaches vary from corporate-wide to site-by-site (Aberdeen Group, 2003). However, CAPS Research (2002) reports that purchasing organizations that are involved in service acquisitions, on average, control only 78 percent of expenditures on services versus 91 percent for direct purchases and 81 percent for indirect materials.

Developing Purchasing Strategies

Purchasing strategies have many dimensions such as the

- definition of demand, including the degree of standardization across customers
- solicitation plan
- source selection criteria
- terms and conditions of the contract
- optimal size of the supply base
- nature of the customer-provider relationship.

The optimal choice of these strategies is influenced by a variety of factors, including characteristics of the purchased service (as well as market conditions) and the firm's objectives. For example, the degree of standardization of the purchased service is affected by the diversity of demands for the service across the organization. Firms seek to balance the benefits of standardization across users—greater consistency in services and improved cost control (Avery, 1999)—with the benefits to users of tailoring services to their specific needs.

Similarly, determining the "right" number of suppliers for the company could mean trying to decrease *or* increase the number of suppliers providing a given good or service. A company with too many suppliers might not have sufficient leverage over any individual supplier to reduce costs or increase performance.[3] On the other hand, a company with too few suppliers could be at risk if suppliers do not feel competitive pressure to innovate and improve or if suppliers have difficulty fulfilling their commitments. The "right" number of suppliers will depend on the importance of the good or service to the company, including the risks inherent in interruption of its provision, and the potential for savings through greater consolidation.[4]

---

[3] It is also difficult to form strategic relationships and undertake supplier development activities with a large supply base.

[4] See MacLean (2002) for a discussion of supply base "rationalization."

Figure 2.1 represents one ideal for developing purchasing strategies based on our synthesis of best practices cited in interviews and the literature. Corporate objectives (such as revenue growth and increased market share) help drive what an organization purchases and why. The purchasing organization of the firm in turn develops purchasing objectives (such as cost reductions and increased performance) that are aligned with, and thus support, the overall corporate objectives, and these shape optimal purchasing and supply management strategies for different commodity groups (which can include goods, services, or some combination of the two).

Developing such multifaceted purchasing strategies requires intensive research, the nature of which will be influenced by the characteristics of the service being purchased. When Gene Richter was CPO of IBM, buyers in his organization were required to produce a written procurement strategy for each service category that included an analysis of the worldwide market in order to learn as much as possible about available suppliers, locations of service providers, and their strengths and weaknesses. The written strategy also included an analysis of the strengths and weaknesses of current and anticipated

Figure 2.1
Linkage Between Corporate Objectives and Purchasing Strategies

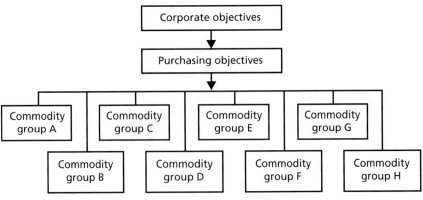

RAND *MG299-2.1*

suppliers and a forecast of future trends (Richter, 2003). American Airlines buyers incorporate market research into their formal commodity strategies as well (MacLean, 2002).[5]

Research on characteristics of internal demand for a service is also important. The level of demand, the diversity of needs at one location or across units at different locations, and the consequences of poor performance of the service must all be understood before a strategy can be developed.[6] The timing of demand—e.g., ongoing service, periodic service, or one-time service—is also important. One of our interviewees emphasized that if a service is going to be purchased only once, the chosen approach to negotiating with and selecting among potential providers might be very different from the approach used if the firm is interested in frequent purchases of the service.

Strategies and Commodity Councils

In our discussions with commercial firms, we learned that cross-functional teams called commodity councils are now being used to develop strategies for managing firm-wide procurement of categories of goods and/or services.[7] In developing its strategy, the goal of a council is to help maximize the firm's competitive advantage by extracting the maximum value for the commodity from its suppliers.[8] Ausink, Baldwin, and Paul (2004) provide an overview of commodity council activities associated with developing procurement strategies.

---

[5] Avery (1999) describes Brunswick Corporation's market research and strategy documentation process.

[6] Brunswick Corporation formally surveys all key users to define internal demand for purchased services (Avery, 1999).

[7] See also Richter (2003) and Duffy and Flynn (2003).

[8] While the goal of a council is to provide a firm-wide approach to purchasing the service, we learned from the literature and the ISM conference that some firms, such as American Airlines and Microsoft, do not mandate that everyone adhere to procurement strategies (MacLean, 2002; Avery, 2003). That is, sometimes units can purchase outside the company-wide strategy. In these cases, however, cost and quality performance should be closely monitored.

Our interviews and the business literature indicated that the membership of a commodity council includes a variety of experts and key stakeholders in the company. It is important to include representatives from different user groups, because requirements for the service may differ by function, administrative division in the company, and geographic location of the using organization.[9] Experts in purchasing/acquisition are obvious choices for membership on the council; however, while the commercial firms we interviewed included purchasing experts on commodity councils, we found that the purchasing experts were often not given the leadership role of the council. Experts in the particular service industry itself were often chosen to chair the council instead because of their knowledge of industry trends, cost drivers, and the supply base. For example, one firm we visited had experienced difficulty managing its travel services. The firm hired a well-known travel industry expert to lead a commodity council and help purchasing managers develop a purchasing strategy that would lead to continuous improvement in provision of the service. Finance and legal experts are other likely candidates for commodity council membership (Avery, 2003).

As noted above, the goal of the commodity council is to develop a strategy that leads to the efficient provision of goods or services that contribute to the achievement of overall corporate objectives. To ensure the alignment of objectives and strategies, some organizations have developed a formal process of linking corporate objectives to business plans at lower organizational levels and even to personal development plans for individual employees. Some firms have created performance incentive approaches that help align the actions of council members with corporate objectives. One firm advocates ranking commodity councils by their performance based on specific metrics (discussed in the next chapter) and then publicizing the rankings widely. Every team member of a given council receives the same performance rating based on that council's ranking, and the rating can

---

[9] See also Duffy and Flynn (2003) and MacLean (2002). Avery (2003) reports that 95 percent of respondents to a recent *Purchasing Magazine* survey include user groups in the strategy development process.

affect the size of annual bonuses as well as future opportunities for promotion.

Achieving corporate objectives and evaluating commodity council performance depend on the establishment of appropriate measures of success. The next chapter discusses commercial practices in using metrics for the purchase of services.

CHAPTER THREE

Commercial Firms' Use of Metrics to Manage Service Procurements

Choosing the right set of purchasing and supply management metrics and performance thresholds to provide the information necessary for decisions affecting purchasing strategies and populating those metrics with reliable data are difficult tasks. The business literature is full of case studies and surveys of firms that are unhappy with their current measurement systems (see, for example, Morgan, 2000; and Monczka, Trent, and Handfield, 2002). In this chapter, we discuss measures that our study participants recommended as providing the information they need to better manage their service expenditures.

The firms we interviewed emphasized the use of results-oriented metrics for purchased services rather than process metrics. They focus on how the outcomes of their purchasing and supply management activities for services support corporate objectives, and they are less concerned about the implementation of specific practices. Some metrics are retrospective assessments of past performance. Others are forward-looking predictors of future problems or successes.

The primary outcome categories include cost, quality, supplier satisfaction, implementation of new initiatives, and special interest issues. These are analogous to the categories of metrics they use to manage their purchased goods.[1] Metrics are also used to manage the

---

[1] An additional outcome category tracked for commodities was technology. In our interviews, this category had less relevance for service expenditures.

internal purchasing organization. In this chapter, we discuss each of these categories and provide examples of metrics.[2]

For both the results-oriented and internal management metrics, it is essential that the chosen metrics and their performance thresholds be aligned with the corporate objectives, or corporate strategy, of the firm. These objectives must be reflected in the metrics reported to high-level management as well as in commodity goals and individual business or action plans. Like the corporate strategy, performance metrics and thresholds must be assessed and modified continuously to ensure that they reflect the goals of the organization.

Results-Oriented Metrics

In this section, we describe each of the five results-oriented categories of metrics in detail.

Cost

The most frequently cited metrics in our interviews were related to cost. As service expenditures have increased in prominence, firms have become more interested in assessing and taking advantage of opportunities to reduce the prices paid as well as their total ownership cost for purchased services. Cost metrics varied across firms, but they were clearly oriented toward tracking reductions in costs or tracking cost savings. The three basic types of cost metrics shown in Table 3.1 were discussed in our interviews.

One firm tracks savings measured as reductions in costs. Reductions can be calculated in several ways. Current costs can be compared to costs in the previous period (e.g., the previous year) provided that adjustments are made for inflation as well as changes in the nature of services purchased (Shirley, Ausink, and Baldwin, 2004). An alternative is comparing costs among divisions or regions within the

---

[2] See also Monczka, Trent, and Handfield (2002) for a detailed discussion of a variety of metrics related to purchasing and supply management activities and organizations.

Table 3.1
Cost Metrics

Cost Metrics	Description
Reduced costs (via prices)	Costs relative to previous year
	Costs relative to other divisions or units
	Costs relative to other regions
Change in costs versus change in market index	Change in firm costs for an individual type of service relative to change in a market cost index for that service
Return on investment	Dollar savings divided by procurement spending

firm. In this type of benchmarking activity, the firm compares costs for a particular service to the cost of that service in other divisions within the firm to assess whether there are opportunities to reduce costs. Adjustments are made for regional variation in prices or other market conditions.[3]

Two firms noted that it is necessary to account for exogenous market conditions (that is, those that are not influenced by the firm's actions) when evaluating the performance of the purchasing organization with respect to cost. For example, the cost of programming services rose sharply during much of the 1990s, independent of the actions of any particular firm. Rather than looking only at each firm's change in cost, these companies emphasized that cost metrics should account for market factors that affect costs. For example, cost savings are measured as the internal change in cost (relative to those costs last year) compared to the change in the relevant market cost index. The comparison is made at the individual service level. The goal of each service commodity council within the purchasing organization is to beat the market index for that service.

Table 3.2 illustrates the calculation of this metric for two hypothetical services. In this example, the market cost index for Service A increased 5 percent during the period, and the firm's costs for this

---

[3] Adjustments for differences in the nature of services purchased need to be made in this type of comparison as well.

Table 3.2
Illustrative Example of Calculating Cost Changes
Relative to Indices

	Market Cost Index Change	Firm Cost Change	Metric "Savings"
Service A	+5%	+3%	+2%
Service B	–5%	–8%	+3%

service increased 3 percent. Thus, the procurement team achieved a net savings of 2 percent. Likewise, the market cost index for Service B decreased by 5 percent and the procurement team achieved reductions in costs of 8 percent, leading to net savings of 3 percent.

This type of metric allows firms to account for changes in market conditions, particularly prices, when assessing the performance of their purchasing organizations. The individual service procurement teams for one of the firms we interviewed tend to "beat" the index for all of the firm's purchases. To provide an incentive for cost savings, procurement teams for individual services are ranked against each other based on this metric (i.e., the savings they achieved relative to the market index). In the above example, the procurement team for Service A would rank lower than the procurement team for Service B because it achieved a lower percentage of savings.

It is important to note that this metric ignores the absolute cost of a product in part because such comparisons can be confounded by nonprice concerns. For example, a market index might indicate a price level of $20 for a particular product or service. However, the price paid by a firm for the product or service might be higher. Higher prices are acceptable if they are justified by some required specialization or other nonprice concern. The concentration on metrics that measure the rates of change within the firm relative to the rate of change in the market index helps control for such confounding factors.

One interviewee told us that, ideally, the cost metric discussed above should benchmark the firm's costs or changes in costs not against the general market index, but rather against the costs of the firm's nearest competitors. However, such a comparison is generally impossible because information about how much competitors are paying for similar products or services is carefully guarded. This type of comparison is possible only in special circumstances such as the merger of two former competitors.

A third cost metric is the return on investment (ROI) for procurement strategies, which measures the cost benefits associated with implementation of new aspects of procurement strategies. These can include implementation of new practices and acquiring new skills through training and hiring programs. The ROI is measured as the reduction in expenditures divided by the cost of new procurement activities that led to the realized savings. Based on his experience, one CPO indicated that he strives for a three-to-one ratio between cost savings and investments in improving his organization's procurement capabilities, although lower levels of benefits could still be used to justify investments. This measure provides a financial justification for desired new procurement activities, which typically struggle for resources, particularly within firms seeking to reduce their cost structure. It can also serve as a measure of the effectiveness of the procurement strategy and implementation.

Implementation Considerations. Effective implementation of cost metrics requires that comparisons be valid and informative. Although used successfully by the commercial firms we surveyed, the metrics presented above pose considerable implementation challenges.

Each of the cost measures in Table 3.1 is based on a comparison of costs—across time, divisions, and/or regions. Comparing costs of services over time works best for those services that are purchased frequently or on an ongoing basis, which ensures that the firm has sufficient data for comparison. For periodic or one-time purchases, data are often insufficient to make valid comparisons. In order for the comparison across time to be informative, the firm must account for changes in what they bought over time and in market conditions. For example, changes in the service purchased may include changes in service scale (e.g., number of square feet cleaned), scope (e.g., adding recycling to a refuse contract), or the level of quality (e.g., faster response times) (see Shirley, Ausink, and Baldwin, 2004). Changes in market conditions might include inflation or technological advances that affect the price, as discussed above. Index-based measures provide a way to help control for these. Comparisons across divisions or regions are also complicated by differences in local market conditions.

Calculating changes in costs over time and controlling for these factors require detailed data on service purchases. Firms must be able to track what they bought and how much they paid and also be able to disaggregate those purchases by service type, time, and region. This requirement can be a significant impediment to implementation of performance metrics. The firms we interviewed struggled to track service expenditures adequately during the initial stages of implementing performance metrics for their purchasing organizations. These firms implemented additional internal data collection procedures, such as new information systems (e.g., Ariba, Elance, and Peoplesoft), to ensure that cost metrics could be populated.[4]

Some measures, such as the market index comparison, also require firms to collect data from external sources. For service purchases, firms track changes in prices using data from public and private sources. Public data sources include compensation data from the Bureau of Labor Statistics. Firms also purchased market data from private providers and industry sources such as Gartner, ISUPPLI.com, and Mercer Consulting. For any chosen source, the important characteristics are relevance to the firm's purchases and independence so that the indices are not influenced by the firm's actions.[5]

The firms we interviewed calculate cost metrics for individual types of services. In order to create an overarching cost metric, the cost performance of individual types of services can be aggregated to the firm level. Not all services are given equal weight in the aggregate metric. Rather, the aggregate cost metric weights individual services by some measure to take into account the relative importance of each

---

[4] See Jones (2003) for more discussion of information systems and providers.

[5] In one firm, procurement agents who were evaluated based on these indices were involved in the selection of the market indices used for comparisons. However, they were not allowed to change the relevant index midyear.

service in the firm's overall expenditures. Often firms use weights corresponding to the individual service's share of expenditures.

Quality

The second most often cited category of metrics was quality.[6] Quality is a difficult concept to measure for services. Unlike goods purchases, simple metrics such as the percentage of defective products are not relevant for services.[7] Among the firms we interviewed, service quality is most often measured in terms of whether the end user or demander of the service was satisfied (i.e., customer satisfaction) or in terms of reliability of the service (see Table 3.3).

Customer satisfaction is measured for overall performance as well as performance among specific dimensions that are important to customers (e.g., responsiveness). For ongoing or continuous services such as telecommunications or network access, service reliability may be tracked through the number of service interruptions. Another in-

Table 3.3
Quality Metrics

Quality Metrics	Description
Customer satisfaction ratings	Responses from customer satisfaction survey regarding • overall satisfaction • satisfaction with specific dimensions of performance
Service reliability	Frequency of service interruptions
	Continuity of service

---

[6] Krowinski and Steiber (1996) quote management expert Peter F. Drucker as saying that acquiring a customer comes first, then retaining the customer, and finally maximizing profitability from the relationship with the customer. High quality is important for retaining a customer, and though Krowinski and Steiber focus on the benefits of high customer satisfaction in the health care business, other organizations find analogous benefits in high-quality service.

[7] Smeltzer and Ogden (2002) discuss measuring the quality of purchased services versus materials.

dicator of service continuity is the number of days before a key posi-tion is filled, for example, in a facilities call center operation.

Implementation Considerations. Like cost metrics, there are also data challenges for quality metrics. Data needed for these measures are generally not captured by standard internal data systems. Firms we interviewed use surveys of service consumers to gather data on customer satisfaction and service reliability.[8] Designing and imple-menting effective customer satisfaction surveys is a complex and challenging task. The quality of the data depends on many factors, including the size and quality of the sample (i.e., did it target the most appropriate personnel), question wording and response format.[9]

The timing of the survey is also quite important and depends on the frequency of purchases for that service. For services that are on-going or are purchased often, data are collected on a periodic basis (e.g., semiannually). In one case of ongoing services (e.g., call cen-ters), one firm supplements customer surveys with spot checks of quality by, for example, having a quality assurance person monitor a phone call to see how well a customer is served. Data collection is more difficult for services that are purchased infrequently or on a one-time basis (e.g., consulting services); in these cases, customer sat-isfaction can be measured, but it should be done immediately after service completion.

Interviewees also noted complications in interpreting customer satisfaction ratings because of potential differences between what pro-viders were asked to do and customer expectations for those services. To facilitate the measurement of quality for services, interviewees noted that there must be clearly stated expectations about the desired outcome of service provision and that these expectations must be

---

[8] American Airlines surveys users to construct supplier performance ratings. Survey results are sent to high-level executives within the supplier organizations (MacLean, 2002). Bruns-wick Corporation surveys customers quarterly. If a supplier performs poorly for three con-secutive quarters, Brunswick cancels the contract with no penalty to itself (Avery, 1999).

[9] Quality can be a function of both the intrinsic merit of a service and the match between the service and the organization's requirements. Customer satisfaction surveys are more likely to yield actionable findings if the questions are worded to capture these distinctions. We thank our RAND colleague Chris Nelson for raising this issue.

communicated to all customers. Otherwise, customers may have inappropriate expectations that lead to distortions in satisfaction ratings.[10] Customer representation on commodity councils can also help mitigate these problems.

Like the cost metrics, quality metrics are evaluated separately for each type of service. To generate an overall quality metric, the performance of individual services can be aggregated to the firm level through a weighting scheme, such as the relative importance of each service in the firm's overall expenditures.

Supplier Satisfaction

A third type of metric viewed by interviewees as important is supplier satisfaction with the customer. The purpose of a supplier satisfaction assessment is to ensure that the buying firm continues to be able to conduct business with the best suppliers. Thus, this is primarily a forward-looking metric. Interviewees noted that access to good suppliers is critical to their firms' future success. One interviewee indicated that it is particularly important to know how suppliers view the buying firm relative to the firm's competitors. Richter (2003) recommends that a buying firm should seek to be viewed as one of its supplier's best customers, not necessarily the easiest. Table 3.4 lists two types of supplier satisfaction metrics discussed in interviews.

Table 3.4
Supplier Satisfaction Metrics

Supplier Satisfaction Metrics	Description
Supplier satisfaction ratings	Responses from supplier satisfaction survey • Overall satisfaction • Satisfaction with specific dimensions of interactions • Satisfaction with different parts of the buying organization
Complaints	Supplier-initiated concerns

---

[10] See also Duffy and Flynn (2003).

In addition to overall supplier satisfaction, buying firms may be interested in suppliers' assessments of their performance in important dimensions such as fairness and communication, as well as the performance of different parts of the buying firm's organization, e.g., direct service users or contract managers. Rather than surveying the supplier as a monolithic entity, one firm tailors its survey components to different parts of the supplier's organization. All units within the supplier that interact with the purchasing firm are targeted by some component of the survey. For example, both the engineering department and the sales department at the supplier would receive some component of the survey. The components are essential in diagnosing the source of potential problems with supplier relations.

Another measure of supplier satisfaction is the number of complaints made against the firm by the supplier. One firm we interviewed employs an ombudsman to field internal and external complaints. Anonymous complaints are encouraged in order to assure the supplier that there will be no retribution.

Implementation Considerations. Ratings of supplier satisfaction are constructed from data collected via surveys of suppliers. These surveys can be conducted in-house by the buying firm or by a third party. Third-party surveys ensure confidentiality and may encourage more-honest responses from suppliers.

Supplier surveys can be costly for both the buying firm and suppliers. One interviewee indicated that the firm's survey cost approximately $200,000 to construct and implement. These surveys can be very time-consuming for buyers and suppliers as well. To minimize the financial and time costs, the firms conduct supplier surveys only annually or biennially. Firms may rotate the surveys through their suppliers, surveying only a portion of their supply base each time. For example, one firm conducts a survey of half of its suppliers each year; the other half of the supply base is surveyed the following year. This rotation allows them to collect an annual measure of supplier satisfaction while burdening individual suppliers only biennially.

New Initiatives

A fourth category of metrics focuses on tracking and supporting implementation of specific initiatives to improve outcomes of purchased services. Examples of such initiatives include supply base rationalization (i.e., creating a supply base that is the right size and composition), supplier development, and the development of personnel with more sophisticated purchasing and supply management skills (discussed below).

Interviewees were careful to distinguish between process and outcome metrics when measuring implementation of specific initiatives. Process metrics are used to track progress with specific parts of an implementation plan, and thus are forward looking. Outcome metrics are used to measure initiative results against prespecified goals. As an example, for a supplier development initiative, process metrics might track the number of people working on these efforts and the number of projects under way at a point in time. Outcome metrics may track whether expected savings or performance improvements were achieved. Table 3.5 provides illustrative examples of initiative metrics based on our interviews.

Implementation Considerations. Developing initiatives, implementation plans, goals, and their associated metrics is a challenging, time-consuming process. For example, analyses of firm expenditures

Table 3.5
Illustrative Initiative Metrics

Example Initiative	Potential Process Metrics	Potential Outcome Metrics
Supply base rationalization	Reductions in nonstrategic suppliers Reductions in sole-source situations	Savings Responsiveness Customer satisfaction
Supplier development	Number of people involved Number of projects	Savings Improved performance
Personnel development	Number of training hours per year, per employee	Mastery of desired skills

and supply chain risks are necessary to determine the right approach and goals for supply base rationalization. Implementation schedules and desired outcomes must be realistic in order for initiative metrics to be helpful and meaningful. In addition, process metrics should include information that can be used to refine the plan during implementation if results are less positive than desired.

For metrics not included in other categories discussed above, firms undertake special collection efforts to support the initiative.

Special Interest

The final category of results-oriented metrics described by interviewees tracks issues of special interest to the buying firm. Special interest metrics may encompass external or internal concerns. For example, special interest metrics might track the amount or percentage of spending the firm directs to small or minority-owned businesses (through prime contracts alone or including both prime and subcontracts) or the frequency and severity of workplace safety and security incidents. Table 3.6 describes these metrics.

Table 3.6
Special Interest Metrics

Special Interest Metrics	Description
Support of small or minority-owned businesses	Dollars spent with these firms Percentage of expenditures with these firms
Safety and security	Frequency of safety incidents Frequency of security incidents

Internal Management Metrics

In addition to results-oriented metrics, commercial firms also use performance metrics to monitor and improve management of their purchasing organizations. These inward-focused metrics complement the high-level effectiveness metrics discussed above. Interviewees indi-

Table 3.7
Internal Management Metrics

Internal Management Metrics	Description
Internal customer satisfaction	Dollars spent outside the corporate strategies (maverick buying)
	Satisfaction rating based on internal customer surveys
Personnel training and retention	Process: Number of training hours per employee per year. Outcome: Mastery of desired skills
	Retention of high-quality employees
Ethics violations	Number of violations per year

cated that their firms track internal customer satisfaction, training and retention of personnel, and adherence to procurement ethics policies. These are summarized in Table 3.7 and are discussed below.

Internal Customer Satisfaction

Internal customer satisfaction metrics evaluate how well the purchasing organization is meeting the needs of its internal customers. These customers are the firm's business units that utilize (or should utilize) the procurement organization's services to buy the goods and services they need. This metric is both retrospective—how well the organization performed in the past—and forward-looking—an indicator of how effective the organization will be in shaping corporate purchasing in the future. The commercial firms in our sample tracked internal customer satisfaction using both indirect and direct evidence.

The prevalence of so-called "maverick" buying can be used as an indirect measure of internal customer satisfaction. Maverick buying is the amount of buying (measured in dollars) that circumvents the corporate purchasing strategy, e.g., making travel arrangements on one's own instead of using the corporate travel department and agreements, potentially leading to increased purchase costs. Significant levels of such ad hoc buying could indicate that there is some dissatisfaction with the purchasing organization, the purchasing strategy, or its implementation. Individual purchases must be analyzed to determine the source of the problem. For example, when FedEx's purchasing department became bogged down with paperwork and unresponsive to its internal customers, service users began dealing directly with providers, often without receiving the discounts that FedEx had already negotiated for those services (Jones, 2003). Alternatively, there may be resistance to a shift from the previous way of doing business to the new approach for purchasing services, e.g., moving from decentralized to centralized purchasing. To counteract maverick buying, one of our interviewees reports the most serious cases—and their associated costs—to top management in order to obtain management's support in aligning customers' actions with the corporate strategy.

Some firms also implement internal surveys to assess satisfaction with the purchasing organization. Surveys are conducted on a periodic basis such as semiannually. One interviewee suggested that the optimal range for customer satisfaction with purchasing was 80 to 90 percent. In his opinion, rankings below 80 percent indicate that there is some failure within the purchasing organization that needs to be addressed. In order to correct the problem, the survey should also provide an opportunity for respondents to describe the reason for their dissatisfaction. Otherwise, unsatisfactory ratings must be investigated to determine the cause. Rankings above 90 percent suggest a different sort of problem. Perhaps the purchasing organization is easily manipulated by internal customers, or internal customers might be doing all the research on their own and using the purchasing department solely as a "clerk" function.

Implementation Considerations. Both of these measures require special data collection efforts. Maverick buying measures are particularly challenging since they require that the firm track expenditures that occur outside the purchasing organization. As long as these expenditures are captured in some sort of purchasing data system, maverick buying can be measured; however, if these expenditures fall outside of these data systems, tracking them becomes virtually impossible.

Internal customer satisfaction surveys could be incorporated into customer satisfaction (with the purchased product) surveys discussed above.

Personnel Training and Retention

Interviewees and ISM conference participants emphasized that an essential element of any purchasing organization's current and future success is the quality and expertise of its personnel. Conducting analyses to design and then implement optimal purchasing strategies requires sophisticated skills. As a result, analyses of required skills relative to current skills and development of individual training plans are explicit elements of the business plan for one purchasing organization we learned about in our interviews.

This firm tracks both process and outcome metrics with respect to training. High-level process metrics track training levels such as the number of training hours per employee per year.[11] Outcome metrics for training track the success of training programs by monitoring how well trainees master required skills. This firm uses professional certifications and assessments of supervisors to indicate mastery.[12]

Retention of high-quality (i.e., highly-trained, effective) personnel is a natural complement to training. Thus, the firm referenced above that has workforce development initiatives also tracks the retention rates of its high-quality personnel.

Implementation Considerations. Evaluating training requirements and training programs and measuring mastery of desired skills are difficult tasks. See Ausink, Baldwin, and Paul (2004) for a discussion of the advantages and disadvantages of alternative skills evaluation and training evaluation procedures.

Even for the most highly valued employees, the optimal staff turnover rate may not be zero percent (100 percent retention). Some turnover is deemed desirable in many cases, for example because of the opportunity to gain new ideas, and there are costs associated with retaining experienced, high-quality staff who are sought after by other

---

[11] Such a high-level training metric aggregates information about individuals' progress toward meeting their own training requirements based on their personal skill development plans.

[12] The United States Postal Service and J.C. Penney went through similar workforce development efforts and used certifications and supervisor/employee assessments to identify needs and measure progress (Strange, 2002; Hanson, 2002). See also Ausink, Baldwin, and Paul (2004) for more discussion about procurement personnel training.

organizations. Indeed, the costs of retaining such employees may exceed the organization costs of replacing them. [See Abelson and Baysinger (1984) and Dalton and Todor (1993).][13]

Ethics Violations

Although interviewees did not indicate that they track adherence to particular purchasing methods or practices (i.e., they care about results, not how those results were achieved), firms do track ethics violations to determine how well purchasing personnel are adhering to the firm's ethics policies, particularly with respect to interactions with suppliers.[14]

Implementation Considerations. Tracking ethics violations is a sensitive endeavor. One interviewee noted that the firm's purchasing organization had an internal ombudsman to field these and other kinds of complaints. Reports of violations can come from other employees or suppliers and may be offered anonymously.

Metrics Baseline Data

In addition to the metrics implementation considerations discussed above, interviewees told us that their firms initially struggled to manage their expenditures on services because of a lack of baseline data for their chosen metrics. Information about the nature of service expenditures (e.g., what was purchased, for how much, from whom) was difficult to collect because internal data sources were often inadequate. In one case, the firm called upon its suppliers to provide needed baseline data about the firm's purchases. One firm was lucky to have some business units that had carefully tracked expenditures for certain services. The firm used these units as a foundation to build on for future data collection efforts.

---

[13] We thank our RAND colleague Nick Castle for making this point.

[14] It may also be possible and desirable to measure the severity of such violations.

Reporting Metrics to High-Level Corporate Management

Purchasing executives report important information about their organizations' activities to their firms' leadership on a regular basis. Interviewees indicated that their firms' corporate managers are primarily interested in cost, quality, and supplier satisfaction metrics. These measures are typically aggregated to the corporate level based on expenditure shares. However, reports on individual services are also encouraged. Particularly successful efforts for individual types of services are highlighted to denote the purchasing organization's progress. One interviewee also highlights so-called missed opportunities, such as the prevalence of maverick buying of goods or services that does not serve the overall corporate strategy and undermines savings efforts. By contrasting missed opportunities with successful efforts, this person gains corporate management's support for efforts to expand the use of successful practices to new areas.

The frequency of reports to corporate management depends on the type of metric. For metrics such as costs, corporate management of firms in our study reviews metrics on a quarterly basis. Internal customer satisfaction metrics may be reported somewhat less frequently (e.g., semiannually). Supplier satisfaction metrics are reported based on the frequency of the survey (and thus may be reported as infrequently as every two years). Particular problem areas (or successes) and special initiative metrics are reported as necessary.

CHAPTER FOUR

Recommendations for the Air Force

The previous two chapters described well-respected commercial practitioners' approaches to measuring and managing the outcomes of purchased services. In this chapter, we describe how the AFPEO/CM could adopt and adapt several of these practices to improve Air Force service outcomes and support for its mission objectives.

The Air Force is not a commercial firm; it is different in important ways. For example, while it is crucial for the Air Force to be fiscally responsible with the taxpayers' money, the ability to perform its mission successfully will always be more important than meeting budget constraints or reducing costs. The Air Force's ability to implement optimal supply strategies is constrained by its obligations to meet a broad range of socioeconomic and other special interest objectives. And it has limited ability to hire experienced personnel who bring needed expertise to positions in the upper tiers of its organizations or to provide incentives to its personnel to align their actions with high-level objectives.

However, the Air Force is in the process of implementing a number of well-respected commercial purchasing and supply management practices, including the use of commodity councils to shape optimal strategies for acquiring and managing categories of goods and services. As part of this process, there are opportunities for the Air Force to benefit from implementation of many of the commercial practices discussed in this report.

Metrics

We view the six categories of metrics described in the previous chapter as a balanced approach to managing service acquisitions and addressing a variety of important dimensions of service acquisition performance, including short- and long-run considerations and external and internal activities. As such, these categories are applicable to both private and public sector organizations that purchase services. In this section, we propose metrics for each category that we believe are most relevant to the responsibilities of the AFPEO/CM.[1] These are summarized in Table 4.1.

To be useful, the proposed metrics require accurate data on a wide range of issues. Similar to commercial firms' experiences, some of these data are available within current Air Force data sets, but many will need to be developed.

After the discussion of metrics for each category, we note some of the challenges the Air Force faces in implementing them.

Cost

While cost is clearly the most important category for the commercial firms that we interviewed, our conversations with the AFPEO/CM and his staff indicate that reducing the cost of purchased services is less important than ensuring that those services support Air Force mission needs. However, given the magnitude of Air Force expenditures on services and the potential for cost savings (without hurting performance) through strategic, centralized approaches to purchasing and supply management, cost metrics are an important part of measuring the health of Air Force service acquisitions. We propose three metrics for this category.

---

[1] Procurement personnel training and ethics issues, two internal management topics of interest for commercial firms (as noted in Chapter Three), fall within the responsibilities of the Air Force Deputy Assistant Secretary for Contracting. Thus, we do not recommend AFPEO/CM metrics for them.

Table 4.1
Proposed Portfolio of Metrics for the AFPEO/CM

Metrics Category	Potential Metrics
Cost	Change in costs versus change in market index
	Actual versus projected post-study costs for recently completed A-76 studies
	Procurement ROI
Quality	Customer satisfaction with purchased services
	Reliability or continuity of services
Supplier satisfaction	Supplier satisfaction with doing business with the Air Force
New initiatives	Process and outcome metrics for specific initiatives, which may include • purchasing and supply management • management and oversight of acquisition of services process • customer education
Special interest	Compliance • Percentage of service dollars and contracts awarded to different categories of small businesses • Percentage of service contracts that are performance based
	Other • Percentage of A-76 studies or slots that were successfully competed within the required time frame • Number of protests resulting from A-76 awards • Percentage of key staff for A-76 studies that remain in their jobs throughout those studies • Percentage of provider personnel that remain in their jobs for a given period of time
Internal management	Internal customer satisfaction with the Air Force purchasing process and personnel
	Percentage of dollars associated with purchases executed outside the Air Force's preferred strategy (i.e., maverick buying)

Change in Costs Relative to the Appropriate Market Index. This metric is relevant to services that have already been outsourced. Ideally, it is based on total ownership costs, rather than prices paid, to take into account the additional costs associated with procuring and managing the performance of the services. Even if the absolute level of cost is not of primary concern, the Air Force should be interested in the change in its service acquisition costs over time, relative to the broader market as a whole. As discussed in the previous chapter, the Air Force could obtain market trend data from private sector sources. In addition, Bureau of Labor Statistics indices for specific types of labor can be used as a proxy since labor is a primary input to services. For services whose costs are driven by the purchase of associated goods (e.g., parts for repairs), indices for those goods could be used to supplement the labor indices.[2]

As discussed in Chapter Three, measuring changes in the cost of purchased services over time is difficult because of the potential for changes in the nature of the services purchased (i.e., scale, scope, or quality). Shirley, Ausink, and Baldwin (2004) describe a methodology to control for such changes, to the extent possible, in cost calculations.

This measure should be tracked for individual categories of services and then aggregated across types of services by weighting the service-specific metrics by the proportion of expenditures associated with each.

Actual Versus Projected Post-Study Costs for Recently Completed A-76 Studies. For services that have been subject to competition through A-76 studies, the AFPEO/CM may want to track the actual versus the projected post-study costs of those services to ensure that the Air Force is realizing the anticipated benefits from the competition. It is important to measure this for both the services that are retained in house—performed by the winning government organization, called the most efficient organization (MEO)—as well as those that are outsourced to the private sector.

Once the new commercial provider or government organizational structure has been in place for a while, the measure discussed above for tracking changes in costs of outsourced services relative to market indices should be used.

---

[2] We recognize that there is a great deal of discussion within the Air Force about whether repair is a service or a good.

This measure also should be tracked for individual categories of services and aggregated across types of services by weighting the service-specific metrics by the proportion of expenditures associated with each.

Procurement ROI. Commercial experience suggests that as the Air Force implements commodity councils and other well-respected purchasing and supply management practices, it will need to make investments in its procurement personnel, organizations, and activities. Such investments may include training to develop the skills needed to design and implement more sophisticated purchasing and supply management activities, enhancing the workforce by hiring personnel with specific technical skills (such as service industry experts), and so forth. To justify these investments, the Air Force could measure the cost savings benefits associated with specific types of investments and compare them to the investment cost.

An alternative approach is to measure the net effectiveness of Air Force procurement in reducing service acquisition costs, i.e., achieved savings versus the procurement organization's budget.

Existing Data. These recommended cost metrics require detailed information about the costs incurred by the Air Force over time for purchased services; market indices; A-76 baseline, projected, and realized costs; and the cost of new procurement activities.

For previously outsourced services, the Air Force has some information about expenditures for services on a contract-by-contract basis within the DD350 database.[3] However, we have concerns about the quality of those data, specifically their ability to accurately capture the full range of services the Air Force purchases and their contract costs (Dixon et al., forthcoming). In addition, the DD350 database does not include all transactions. Contract actions for less than $25,000[4] and government purchase card expenditures are tracked in

---

[3] This database tracks descriptive information such as the good or service purchased, the dollar amount, and the supplier for virtually all contract transactions greater than $25,000.

[4] Some of the smaller actions can be found in the DD350 database, but they are not recorded there systematically. Most of these small transactions are aggregated monthly in the DD1057 system.

separate systems with less detail. Furthermore, to our knowledge, the Air Force does not currently track the total ownership cost of purchased services.

Indices for labor categories are publicly available from the Bureau of Labor Statistics, and these could be useful for comparing cost changes to those in the commercial sector. Other service-specific indices would have to be purchased from private sector sources.

For A-76 studies, the Air Force has information about the pre-study costs of the affected activities, the proposed costs of the winning bidder (contractor or MEO), and the post-study realized cost of any outsourced services. These data may not be as detailed and accurate as desired, but they are readily available. However, the Air Force has not been tracking the actual post-study costs of winning MEOs in the same way. The new A-76 study guidelines require federal agencies to more carefully track the performance of winning MEOs. It is hoped that these post-study cost data will be collected systematically as part of this process.

Quality

Because of its link to Air Force mission, the quality of purchased services may be the most important category of metrics for the AFPEO/CM. We propose two quality metrics.

Customer Satisfaction with Purchased Services. As described in the previous chapter, customer satisfaction with services is typically assessed through some type of survey. Satisfaction ratings can be constructed for specific contracts or types of services and then aggregated into comprehensive measures by weighting ratings according to the percentage of expenditures they represent.

Prior to assessing customer satisfaction, the AFPEO/CM will need to identify relevant customer organizations across the Air Force. It may be helpful to seek feedback from Air Force leadership to identify these groups. When assessing satisfaction with a service procured to support an installation, the AFPEO/CM may want to include base commanders, technical experts who help define requirements and assess contractor performance, and base occupants who benefit from the service. The AFPEO/CM will also need to make sure that information about expected levels of performance is communicated broadly to customers to ensure that customer assessments are appropriate and consistent with contractual agreements.

Writing good survey questions is always challenging. However, there are resources that can help, including web sources.[5] Surveys may use a numeric scale (e.g., ratings from one to ten) to measure the level of satisfaction and/or allow open-ended comments and suggestions. Prior RAND research suggests that firms have varying philosophies about conducting internal customer satisfaction surveys (Baldwin, Camm, and Moore, 2000; Baldwin and Hunter, 2004). Firms differ in the frequency of surveys, the percentage of customers surveyed, and the types of surveys used. For services performed only once or infrequently, surveys should closely follow provision of the service. For frequent or ongoing services, a useful approach might be to conduct surveys every six months, randomly selecting representatives from approximately 25–50 percent of customer organizations for each survey (so that all customer organizations are surveyed once every one to two years). Web-based surveys may also significantly reduce the costs of conducting a survey.[6] Surveys can be performed by Air Force procurement personnel or by third-party consultants.

Survey response rates are a concern, so it would be wise to seek feedback from customers on any proposed approach prior to implementation. The ease of making detailed comments in a web-based format may help increase the willingness of customers to participate. Also, as part of a prior study, we learned of a commercial firm that increased its response rates by offering an incentive for participating: All respondents were entered into a raffle, with a chance to win a small gift.

Reliability or Continuity of Services. For frequently performed or continuous services, such as cell phone service or network access, service reliability or continuity can directly affect the Air Force's abil-

---

[5] A web search on "customer satisfaction surveys" yielded many web sites, including QuestionPro.com.

[6] There are web sites that can facilitate creation and implementation of web-based surveys, e.g., SurveyMonkey.com.

ity to accomplish its mission. Sometimes reliability can be captured by service-specific measures such as the percentage of time a service was available when needed. Otherwise, it could be captured through a customer satisfaction survey, specifically examining reliability as a component of performance.

Existing Data. Currently, the Air Force does not formally and systematically collect the kinds of customer satisfaction data that commercial firms value. However, it does track information on the past performance of service providers within the Contractor Performance Assessment Reporting System database. This information is typically determined by Air Force personnel involved in management of individual contracts and is based on performance against formal metrics and other assessments. As such, ideally, it should be correlated with customer satisfaction with purchased services. However, we believe it would be better to obtain these data directly from users through a survey. Such customer satisfaction data would represent a greater breadth of customers and their concerns, and the ratings could be tailored to focus on specific dimensions of performance.

Supplier Satisfaction

The Air Force, like commercial firms, benefits from doing business with the best, most capable suppliers of services. These include (1) providers of commercial-like services, such as installation support, that offer needed levels of performance at reduced costs (with continuous improvement initiatives potentially leading to better performance and/or further cost reductions over time) and (2) providers of mission capabilities that offer technological or other types of advances that help the Air Force maintain its advantage against adversaries. Becoming a better buyer from providers' perspectives can help the Air Force gain and retain access to desired firms. We propose one metric for this category: supplier surveys.

The Air Force sometimes seeks input from its major contractors about how policies affect the way these firms do business. However, it does not currently collect data on supplier satisfaction in any systematic way. Surveying suppliers would provide useful information for improving Air Force procurement of services. Such a survey would seek to determine suppliers' perspectives about how easy it is to do business with the Air Force, what actions the Air Force could take to help develop or enhance mutually beneficial strategic partnerships, whether Air Force procurement personnel are treating suppliers fairly, and so forth. Ideally, different parts of the survey should target different divisions within suppliers' organizations. Because suppliers deal with many different parts of the Air Force, such a survey could also be used to identify successful practices and lessons from among individual internal Air Force buying organizations that could be shared more widely across the Air Force.

Given the intricacies of similar surveys found in the commercial sector, the Air Force may want to utilize a third-party consultant to help design and implement the survey, at least initially. The costs will need to be weighed against the benefits when determining the best frequency and the number of suppliers chosen for the survey. The Air Force could consider initially surveying firms biennially (either all at once or 50 percent of providers each year) and targeting its most important suppliers first, i.e., those that provide services the Air Force spends a lot of money on or services that are important for mission execution. It may also want to include a random selection of other suppliers. As the Air Force gains experience with this practice, it may want to increase or decrease the number of firms surveyed or the survey frequency based on the results of prior surveys or timing of any new initiatives that may affect supplier satisfaction.

Initiatives and New Policies

This category of metrics would be used to track implementation of initiatives and policies of particular interest to the AFPEO/CM. Both outcome-oriented and process-oriented metrics are important so that the AFPEO/CM can track progress against goals and adjust implementation as needed. The specific metrics tracked should evolve over time to reflect experience with past efforts and any new initiatives. Currently, the following may be of interest to the AFPEO/CM: implementation of well-respected commercial purchasing and supply management practices such as performing in-depth market research or writing outcome-oriented statements of work, implementation of the Management and Oversight of Acquisition of Services Process, and efforts to educate internal Air Force customers on the appropriate procurement process.

Outcome-oriented metrics for specific initiatives will likely focus on improvements in some dimension(s) of quality and/or cost of purchased services. Thus, the metrics discussed above are relevant here as well.

Process-oriented implementation metrics are challenging. To be useful, they must capture actions taken and the quality and/or appropriateness of those actions. Simply tracking whether a new practice was used or a new policy was followed does not provide sufficient information. There may be situations in which certain practices are inappropriate, and there are different ways to "use" a practice or apply a policy that result in different qualities of outcomes. For example, when performing market research, one could use the phone book to identify local suppliers and make phone calls from the office. Alternatively, one could do intensive research drawing on respected trade journals, participate in trade conferences, or make site visits to prospective suppliers' customers. The fact that these very different approaches to implementation are appropriate in different circumstances or for different types of services complicates measurement further still.

An ideal process-oriented metric tracks the percentage of procurement activities for which the practice or policy was appropriate and was followed. Ideally, this metric is supported by data from two sources: (1) self-reports provided by the responsible procurement professionals and (2) periodic evaluations performed by independent experts to validate whether their actions were appropriate for the circumstances. The evaluations are most useful and consistent if they are conducted by a single group of independent experts. However, evaluations by supervisors of the responsible personnel are less costly to support and can provide useful information as well. See Ausink, Baldwin, and Paul (2004) for details about these and related measurement issues.

Data needs for these metrics will vary depending on the issues of interest.

Special Interest

As with initiatives and new policies, the AFPEO/CM needs the ability to monitor information on special interest issues. In this section, we describe a few metrics related to important issues that we have heard discussed within the AFPEO/CM and Air Force contracting communities. As such, we hope that these metrics are both relevant and illustrative; however, we do not view this as a comprehensive list.

Some issues are of interest to the AFPEO/CM because of Air Force obligations to comply with external mandates. For example, Congress has mandated that the Department of Defense award 23 percent of its contract dollars directly to small businesses (as well as specific subcategories such as small disadvantaged businesses).[7] Because small businesses provide many services to the Air Force, the AFPEO/CM may want to monitor the *percentage of service dollars and contracts awarded to different categories of small businesses.*

In Chapter One we described the requirements for the Air Force to implement performance-based service contracts and the AFPEO/CM's role in this implementation. Thus, the AFPEO/CM will also need to monitor the *percentage of service contracts that are performance based* to track progress toward meeting these goals. Implementation of performance-based practices requires discretion to appropriately align the approach with the nature of the service requirements; thus, this type of metric has the same measurement challenges discussed above.

Other potential issues of interest include the following. The current administration strongly supports federal agencies opening a portion of their personnel slots associated with commercial-like activities to competition with private sector firms through A-76 studies. The AFPEO/CM is responsible for execution of A-76 studies that include more than 300 slots and thus may want to monitor the *percentage of A-76 studies or slots that were successfully competed within the required time frame.* Similarly, the AFPEO/CM may want to track the *number*

---

[7] See the DoD Office of Small and Disadvantaged Business Utilization web site for more information about DoD goals. Online at http://www.acq.osd.mil/sadbu/index.html (as of October 12, 2004).

of protests resulting from A-76 awards (broken down by MEO and contractor) because these protests can delay awards and disrupt the provision of services to Air Force consumers. In addition, the participation of key Air Force personnel performing services that are being competed through A-76 studies is critical for successful execution of those studies. Thus, the AFPEO/CM may want to track the *percentage of key staff for A-76 studies that remain in their jobs throughout those studies.* On a related note, for force protection reasons, the Air Force may be concerned about the possibility of frequent turnover among supplier personnel providing services at Air Force locations.[8] Therefore, the AFPEO/CM may want to track the *percentage of provider personnel that remain in their jobs for a given period of time.*

Existing Data. The Air Force already tracks much of the data needed for the recommended special interest metrics. The DD350 and DD1057 databases contain information on contract dollars spent directly (versus through subcontracts) with different categories of small businesses. Our impression from interviews with Air Force contracting officers is that these data receive considerable scrutiny by the small business community; so they are probably some of the most accurate data on Air Force contracts. The DD350 database also tracks the use of performance-based contracts for services; however, we are less optimistic about the accuracy of this information.

For A-76 studies, the Commercial Activity Management Information System database contains information about ongoing and completed studies. Among other information, this system tracks nominated studies, milestones for execution of the studies, and the ultimate outcome (Keating, 1997). The General Accounting Office (GAO) maintains files on A-76 protests. However, to our knowledge, few, if any, data are collected in any systematic fashion on personnel retention for Air Force personnel involved in A-76 studies or provider personnel.

---

[8] As noted in Chapter Three, zero percent turnover in provider personnel is probably not desirable either.

Internal Management

The last category of metrics focuses on the effectiveness of Air Force purchasing organizations' activities, that is, how well they are meeting the service acquisition needs of their internal Air Force customers. This is also an indicator of how effective these organizations will be in the future as they seek to truly transform Air Force purchasing.

We recommend two related metrics here. The first is *internal customer satisfaction with the purchasing process and personnel,* measured through an internal survey as discussed in the previous chapter. The second metric is the *percentage of dollars associated with purchases executed outside of the Air Force's preferred strategy (i.e., maverick buying).* As service commodity councils begin devising optimal purchasing and supply management strategies, the second metric would track the amount of service expenditures that fall outside of these strategies. As noted in Chapter Three, one of our interviewees referred to these as "missed opportunities." This metric should be measured for each category of services and then aggregated by weighting according to the size of Air Force expenditures in those categories.

Existing Data. As part of its ongoing procurement transformation, the Air Force contracting community discussed surveying its customers to learn how well their needs are supported. To our knowledge, this is still planned but has not yet been implemented; information about customers' satisfaction with the purchasing process and personnel is not currently available.

Maverick buying can be difficult to measure. As the Air Force implements its commodity councils for services, it will have an opportunity to begin analyzing purchases by commodity area. To the extent that purchases are captured in the DD350 database, the description of the purchase may allow the commodity council to track total expenditures in the commodity area and then compare those to the purchases that are executed according to the chosen commodity strategy.

Overarching Data Issue

In addition to the data needs and issues discussed above, we are concerned about a lack of detailed information about the types of services the Air Force purchases. The DD350 database is the primary source of this information and provides a single data field for each contract action to describe what is purchased. In a related research study (Dixon et al., forthcoming), RAND surveyed over 100 contracting officers to collect supplemental information for over 200 FY02 Air Force contract actions found in the DD350 database. Our survey results suggest that the single data field describing what is purchased through contract actions is not always sufficient to fully describe a purchase. As a result, some service expenditures are hidden. In other cases, the information provided in the DD350 does not accurately describe the purchase. Without accurate and complete information about which services are purchased at what cost, the AFPEO/CM cannot accurately populate many of the metrics discussed above, and more important, the Air Force cannot construct optimal strategies for its purchased services.

However, there are clearly costs to enhancing the quality of contracts data, including enhancing the current data system, providing additional training for those entering the data, increasing the accuracy of entered data, auditing those data, and so forth. The costs of higher-quality data must be balanced against the benefits of better strategies and metrics resulting from the improved data.

Management Approach

Our interviews with well-respected commercial sector purchasing professionals indicate that good metrics are necessary, but not sufficient, to extract the maximum value from purchased services. Rather, metrics are powerful management tools when implemented and utilized within a centralized commodity council framework.

Commodity Councils

Much like large corporations with diverse business units, the Department of Defense and the individual military branches consist of many organizations that have different mission emphases. Each of these organizations purchases services, many of which are common across organizations, e.g., installation support, information technology support, and advisory and assistance services. Currently, the Department of Defense uses a decentralized approach for purchasing many services. For example, in the Air Force, installation support services are primarily purchased at the local base level. For weapon systems, management support services (e.g., advisory, assistance, and engineering support) are primarily purchased by individual program offices.

However, commercial sector trends as well as public sector experiences with centralized contracts, such as government travel service agreements, suggest that there may be significant opportunities to leverage the military's purchasing power through more strategic, centralized approaches within the Air Force, DoD, or even the federal government.

The DoD is in the process of implementing commodity councils for services that are purchased across the military branches. According to draft plans shared with us, the three proposed service areas are miscellaneous professional services, management advisory services, and miscellaneous and general information technology services. Through analyses of expenditures and other assessments, these councils will be designing optimal strategies for purchasing these services to improve performance and cost outcomes for customers across the DoD. In addition, we believe the expertise developed by these commodity councils may be useful for managing A-76 studies and helping MEOs develop their proposals.

The Air Force purchases many other types of services as well and should consider implementation of its own commodity councils for some of these services. In some cases, it may make sense to combine related goods and services into a single council and construct a joint purchasing strategy for them, e.g., equipment and maintenance support.[9]

---

[9] The Air Force is beginning to implement commodity councils for several categories of goods; see Ausink, Baldwin, and Paul, 2004, for a discussion. The Air Force recently published a concept of operations for commodity councils (U.S. Air Force, 2003).

The membership of the services commodity councils should be tailored to the types of services being purchased. In addition to contracting experts, there are three key categories of members.

Experts on the Service and Its Industry. These are people who understand the details of how the industry works and the drivers of costs for the service. For many services that are not unique to the military, the Air Force does not currently have this type of expertise within its personnel. While information can be acquired through consulting contracts,[10] commercial firms view this knowledge as a core part of their sourcing strategies and maintain this expertise in house. The fastest way to acquire the needed expertise is to hire experts from industry. However, this may be difficult within the Air Force's personnel structure. Alternatively, the Air Force's exchange with industry program can be used to help build this type of knowledge within the Air Force over time.

User Representatives. Representatives of all important user groups (in terms of expenditures or relevance to the mission) for the service should be included on the council. This ensures that the diversity of service requirements is taken into consideration when devising the optimal purchasing and supply management strategy. Depending on the type of service, user groups may include installations, major commands, weapons system program offices, and other defense or government agencies.

Special Interest Representatives. Representatives of special interest groups whose constituents are involved in delivery of the services under consideration should be part of the councils as well. These may include small business advocates for services that are currently provided by significant numbers of small businesses, firms that employ blind and severely handicapped persons,[11] and so forth.

It would be desirable to have a mixture of military and government-employed civilians on the councils to ensure not only that

---

[10] The Air Force's new information technology commodity council has hired consultants to fill this role, at least initially.

[11] The National Industries for the Blind/National Industries for the Severely Handicapped is one such interest group.

"war-fighter" concerns are represented, but also that there is significant continuity in membership and retention of lessons learned over time.

Leadership and Incentives

Our study participants indicated that the Air Force needs strong leadership to successfully improve the management of its purchased services over time. High-level proponents of change can provide help in breaking down resistance to purchasing changes and limiting maverick buying that occurs outside the optimal strategies. Indeed, creation of the AFPEO/CM office is a step in this direction.

It is important for Air Force leadership to communicate the new approach internally at all levels of the organization and to stress that the Air Force is committed to the long-term process of moving toward strategic, more centralized management of service expenditures. External communication to suppliers is needed as well.

Incentives for Air Force personnel and providers could be used to reinforce this commitment to change. As the Air Force implements its commodity councils for services and goods, the performance of these councils should be evaluated relative to their appropriate market indices, customer satisfaction ratings, or other important performance goals. Then councils could be ranked against one another in order of success in meeting goals.[12] These rankings could then be communicated widely throughout the procurement workforce and Air Force leadership.

In addition, it would be helpful to tie individuals' promotion opportunities and, if possible, compensation to their own or their councils' performance. However, even if such formal incentives are not possible, ranking councils and communicating the results can provide powerful informal incentives to meet goals.

The Air Force already has experience tying providers' award fees and contract length to performance, as well as taking past performance into account during source selection decisions for new contracts.

---

[12] This idea is included in the Air Force's concept of operations for commodity councils (U.S. Air Force, 2003).

It may want to consider tying providers' shares of the Air Force's service requirements (i.e., level of business) to their success in meeting key performance goals as well.

Link to Metrics Portfolio

Metrics can be very powerful tools when they provide accurate information that can be acted upon or used to inform important decisions. However, as discussed above, they can be quite costly to implement. Before choosing a specific portfolio of metrics with which to manage Air Force services acquisition, the AFPEO/CM and commodity council leaders should explicitly determine which actions or decisions those metrics are needed to inform. Then metrics should be revisited over time to ensure that they are indeed accomplishing the intended purpose and that they remain aligned with organizational objectives.

Summary

Our research indicates that, like the Air Force, commercial firms are just beginning to pursue strategic, centralized management of their purchased services, and they are basing their approaches for services on their successful approaches for goods. Commercial experiences suggest that a multifaceted management approach—based on commodity councils, guided by a balanced set of performance metrics that reflect important dimensions of performance, and supported by leadership emphasis and incentives—can lead to improved service outcomes and greater value for Air Force buying organizations.

Interview Questions

This appendix contains the interview questions we used to guide our discussions with experts. These questions were provided to interviewees in advance.

Interview Protocol for Chief Purchasing Officers

Background

Before we begin, it would be helpful for us to learn about your background and experience.

How long have you been with this organization? How long have you been in your current position?

What is the size of your purchasing organization—in terms of budget and staff?

Which services has your firm outsourced?

Did you outsource these through many or few contracts?

What is the typical length of your service contracts?

What is the size of your firm's portfolio of service contracts (number of contracts and dollars)?

Metrics

What metrics do you track to determine your purchasing organization's success?
Do you track metrics related to:

> Service contract outcomes (e.g., quality, flexibility, cost)?
> Adherence to purchasing policies, use of desired practices?
> Workforce training and development?

Which metrics are most important to your firm's corporate leaders?

Do you ask your providers for feedback on the quality of your business interactions, e.g., in negotiating a contract or in the day-to-day implementation of the contract?

If so, which metrics do you use to track this feedback?

Are the metrics discussed above your ideal metrics, or are they the best available? Please explain.

> If not ideal, what would be your ideal metrics?

How do you collect data for these metrics?

> Did you implement a special data collection effort for this purpose, or are you able to draw from existing data systems?
> How often do you review these metrics?

If performance is poor in an area, do you have "diagnostic" metrics to help you understand what needs to be addressed in order to improve?

How were your metrics selected?

Was the development of your metrics an iterative process?
How often is the choice of metrics reevaluated?

May we have an example (sanitized, if necessary) of any performance reports compiled by your office?

Can you think of additional metrics that may be useful to the AFPEO/SV? [1]

Roles and Responsibilities of Your Organization

To help us put these metrics in perspective for the AFPEO/SV, it would be useful to better understand your organization's roles and responsibilities.

For the questions below, if your organization is not responsible for these activities, who within your firm is responsible?

Policy

Do you determine or can you influence your firm's services acquisition policies and practices?

Do you determine what services are eligible/appropriate for outsourcing?

Do you determine or can you influence the training program (or job requirements) for personnel involved in purchasing services?

---

[1] At the time of the study, the AFPEO/CM office was called the PEO for Services (AFPEO/SV).

Acquisition Process and Performance

When people (internal or suppliers) have questions about your firm's service contracts or performance of those contracts, do they come to your organization?

Do you oversee your firm's services acquisition processes?

> Are you responsible for ensuring that personnel follow appropriate procedures?
> Does your firm require personnel to obtain waivers to bypass procedures? If so, can you (do you) grant these waivers?
> Are you responsible for implementing improvements in services acquisition processes?
> Are you involved in finalizing work statements, contracts, metrics, and other documents associated with purchasing services?
> Do you determine requirements for data analysis and reporting for your firm's service contracts?

Do you determine the source selection criteria for service contracts?
Do you make final source selection decisions?

Do you participate in formal performance reviews with your firm's service providers?

> How often?
> What information do you examine in these reviews?

Do you determine the level and types of incentives (positive or negative) used in contracts?

> Do you make decisions about incentive awards to providers?

Budget Authority

Can you influence your firm's budget(s) for purchased services and/or allocation of the budget across service areas?

Other Roles and Responsibilities

Do you have other roles and responsibilities associated with your firm's purchased services?

AFPEO/SV Roles and Responsibilities

Can you think of any additional authority, roles, or responsibilities the AFPEO/SV needs in order to be successful in ensuring that the Air Force's large service acquisition activities meet the Air Force's needs?

Additional Information Sources

Do you participate in any professional or trade organizations? If so, which ones?

What other resources do you use to remain informed of advances in best practices (e.g., journals, seminars, meetings, etc.)?

Can you think of other sources of information that might be useful for our study?

Do you have any suggestions for other potential interviewees?

Can you think of anything we should have asked, but didn't?

Interview Protocol for Directors of Services

Background

Before we begin, it would be helpful for us to learn about your background and experience.

How long have you been with this organization? How long have you been in your current position?

What is the size of your services organization—in terms of budget and staff?

Which services have you outsourced?

> Did you outsource these through many or few contracts?
> What is the typical length of your service contracts?

What is the size of your portfolio of service contracts (number of contracts and dollars)?

Metrics

What metrics do you track to determine your services organization's success?

Do you track metrics related to:

> Service contract outcomes (e.g., quality, flexibility, cost)?
> Adherence to service acquisition policies, use of desired practices?
> Workforce training and development?

Which metrics are most important to your firm's corporate leaders?

Do you ask your providers for feedback on the quality of your business interactions, e.g., in negotiating a service contract or in the day-to-day implementation of the contract?

   If so, which metrics do you use to track this feedback?

Are the metrics discussed above your ideal metrics, or are they the best available? Please explain.

   If not ideal, what would be your ideal metrics?

How do you collect data for these metrics?

   Did you implement a special data collection effort for this purpose, or are you able to draw from existing data systems?

How often do you review these metrics?

If performance is poor in an area, do you have "diagnostic" metrics to help you understand what needs to be addressed in order to improve?

How were your metrics selected?

   Was the development of your metrics an iterative process?
   How often is the choice of metrics reevaluated?

May we have an example (sanitized, if necessary) of any performance reports compiled by your office?

Can you think of additional metrics that may be useful to the AFPEO/SV?

Roles and Responsibilities of Your Organization

To help us put these metrics in perspective for the AFPEO/SV, it would be useful to better understand your organization's roles and responsibilities.

For the questions below, if your organization is not responsible for these activities, who within your firm is responsible?

Policy
Do you determine or can you influence your firm's services acquisition policies and practices?

Do you determine what services are eligible/appropriate for outsourcing?

Do you determine or can you influence the training program (or job requirements) for personnel involved in purchasing services?

Acquisition Process and Performance
When people (internal or suppliers) have questions about your firm's service contracts or performance of those contracts, do they come to your organization?

Do you oversee your firm's services acquisition processes?

> Are you responsible for ensuring that personnel follow appropriate procedures?
> Does your firm require personnel to obtain waivers to bypass procedures? If so, can you (do you) grant these waivers?
> Are you responsible for implementing improvements in services acquisition processes?
> Are you involved in finalizing work statements, contracts, metrics, and other documents associated with purchasing services?
> Do you determine requirements for data analysis and reporting for your firm's service contracts?

Do you determine the source selection criteria for service contracts? Do you make final source selection decisions?

Do you participate in formal performance reviews with your firm's service providers?

> How often?
> What information do you examine in these reviews?

Do you determine the level and types of incentives (positive or negative) used in contracts?

> Do you make decisions about incentive awards to providers?

Budget Authority

Can you influence your firm's budget(s) for purchased services and/or allocation of the budget across service areas?

Other Roles and Responsibilities

Do you have other roles and responsibilities associated with your firm's purchased services?

AFPEO/SV Roles and Responsibilities

Can you think of any additional authority, roles, or responsibilities the AFPEO/SV needs in order to be successful in ensuring that the Air Force's large service acquisition activities meet the Air Force's needs?

Additional Information Sources

Do you participate in any professional or trade organizations? If so, which ones?

What other resources do you use to remain informed of advances in best practices (e.g., journals, seminars, meetings, etc.)?

Can you think of other sources of information that might be useful for our study?

Do you have any suggestions for other potential interviewees?
Can you think of anything we should have asked, but didn't?

References

Aberdeen Group, *The Services Supply Chain Automation Benchmark Report: Strategies for a Buckshot Market,* Boston, Mass., June 2003.

Abelson, Michael A., and Barry D. Baysinger, "Optimal and Dysfunctional Turnover: Toward an Organizational Level Model," *The Academy of Management Review,* Vol. 9, No. 2, April 1984, pp. 331–341.

Ausink, John, Laura H. Baldwin, Sarah Hunter, and Chad Shirley, *Implementing Performance-Based Services Acquisition (PBSA): Perspectives from an Air Logistics Center and a Product Center,* Santa Monica, Calif.: RAND Corporation, DB-388-AF, 2002.

Ausink, John, Laura H. Baldwin, and Christopher Paul, *Air Force Procurement Workforce Transformation: Lessons from the Commercial Sector*, Santa Monica, Calif.: RAND Corporation, MG-214-AF, 2004.

Avery, Susan, "Brunswick Saves Big Bucks," *Purchasing*, March 25, 1999, pp. 38–41.

Avery, Susan, "Capture Cost," *Purchasing Magazine Online,* June 19, 2003.

Baldwin, Laura H., Frank Camm, and Nancy Y. Moore, *Strategic Sourcing: Measuring and Managing Performance*, Santa Monica, Calif.: RAND Corporation, DB-287-AF, 2000.

Baldwin, Laura H., and Sarah Hunter, *Defining Needs and Managing Performance of Installation Support Contracts: Perspectives from the Commercial Sector,* Santa Monica, Calif.: RAND Corporation, MR-1812-AF, 2004.

CAPS Research, *Defining and Determining the "Services Spend" in Today's Services Economy,* Tempe, Ariz., September 2002.

CAPS Research, *Managing Your "Services Spend" in Today's Services Economy*, Tempe, Ariz., July 22, 2003.

Cardenas, Anna, "Management and Oversight of the Acquisition of Services Process (MOASP)," briefing, April 22, 2004. Online at http://www.safaq.hq.af.mil/afpeocm/documents/whatwedo_docs/AFPEO_CM_MOASP.ppt (as of October 12, 2004).

Clay, Maureen M., "Oversight and Management Process for Services Acquisitions," Contract Policy Memo 03-C-14, November 26, 2003.

Dalton, Dan R., and William D. Todor, "Turnover, Transfer, Absenteeism: An Interdependent Perspective," *Journal of Management*, Vol. 19, No. 2, 1993, pp. 193–219.

Davis, Tom, Chairman of the House of Representatives Government Reform Subcommittee on Technology and Procurement Policy, Opening Statement for the Hearing on "The Next Steps in Services Acquisition Reform: Learning from the Past, Preparing for the Future," May 22, 2001.

Diernisse, Lisa, "Performance Metrics for Non-Mathematicians," *Contract Management Magazine*, Vol. 43, No. 6, June 2003, pp. 44–53.

Dixon, Lloyd, Chad Shirley, Laura H. Baldwin, John Ausink, Nancy Campbell, *An Assessment of Air Force Data on Contract Expenditures*, Santa Monica, Calif.: RAND Corporation, MG-274-AF, forthcoming.

Duffy, Roberta J., and Anna E. Flynn, "Service Purchases: Not Your Typical Grind," *Inside Supply Management*, Vol. 14, No. 9, 2003, p. 28.

Gansler, Jack S., Under Secretary of Defense (Acquisition and Technology), *Memorandum on Performance-Based Services Acquisition (PBSA)*, April 5, 2000.

General Accounting Office (GAO), *Contract Management: High Level Attention Needed to Transform DOD Services Acquisition*, GAO-03-935, Washington, D.C., September 2003.

General Accounting Office (GAO), *Best Practices: Taking a Strategic Approach Could Improve DoD's Acquisition of Services*, GAO-02-230, Washington, D.C., January 2002.

General Accounting Office (GAO), *Contract Management: Trends and Challenges in Acquiring Services*, GAO-01-753T, Washington, D.C., May 22, 2001.

Hanson, Patricia, Vice President and Director of Purchasing Operations Management, J.C. Penney Co., Inc., "Training: A Common Sense Strategy," presentation at the *3rd Annual ISM Services Group Conference, Smart Business: Leveraging the Services Spend,* Scottsdale, Ariz., December 5–6, 2002.

Jones, Steve, "At Your Service," *Forbes,* March 3, 2003.

Keating, Edward G., *Cancellations and Delays in Completion of Department of Defense A-76 Cost Comparisons,* Santa Monica, Calif.: RAND Corporation, DB-191-OSD, 1997.

Krowinski, William J., and Steven R. Steiber, *Measuring and Managing Patient Satisfaction,* American Hospital Publishing, Inc., 1996.

MacLean, John R., Vice President for Purchasing at American Airlines, "Five Strategies that Really Work," presentation at the *3rd Annual ISM Services Group Conference, Smart Business: Leveraging the Services Spend,* Scottsdale, Ariz., December 5–6, 2002.

Monczka, Robert, Robert Trent, and Robert Handfield, *Purchasing and Supply Chain Management,* Second Edition, South-Western, 2002.

Morgan, Jim, "How Effective Are Your Measurement Systems?" *Purchasing,* December 8, 2000.

Office of Federal Procurement Policy, *Service Contracting,* Policy Letter 91-2, Washington, D.C., April 9, 1991 (rescinded March 30, 2000).

O'Keefe, Sean, *Performance Goals and Management Initiatives for the FY 2002 Budget,* M-01-15, Washington, D.C.: Office of Management and Budget, March 9, 2001.

Phinney, David, "New Contracting Guidelines Favor Performance," *Federal Times,* November 24, 2003.

Richter, Gene, "Ten Private Sector Best Practices," presentation at the Procurement Executive Roundtable sponsored by the SAS Institute, Ritz-Carlton Hotel, Arlington, Va., June 5, 2003.

Shirley, Chad, John Ausink, and Laura H. Baldwin, *Measuring Changes in Service Costs to Meet the Requirements of the 2002 National Defense Authorization Act,* Santa Monica, Calif.: RAND Corporation, MR-1821-AF, 2004.

Smeltzer, Larry R., and Jeffrey A. Ogden, "Purchasing Professionals' Perceived Differences Between Purchasing Materials and Purchasing Services," *The Journal of Supply Chain Management,* Winter 2002, pp. 54–70.

Strange, Keith, Vice President, Supply Management, U.S. Postal Service, "Best Practices in Supply Management Training," presentation at the *3rd Annual ISM Services Group Conference, Smart Business: Leveraging the Services Spend,* Scottsdale, Ariz., December 5–6, 2002.

U.S. Air Force, *Air Force Instruction (AFI) 63-124: Performance-Based Service Contracts (PBSC),* Washington, D.C., February 9, 2004.

U.S. Air Force, *Changes to the Air Force Acquisition Circular (AFAC) 2003-1105,* Washington, D.C., November 5, 2003.

U.S. Congress, 107th Congress (1st Session—2001) National Defense Authorization Act for Fiscal Year 2002, Public Law 107-107, Washington, D.C., October 2, 2001.

U.S. Congress, 107th Congress, 2nd Session, House of Representatives Report 107-772, National Defense Authorization Act for Fiscal Year 2003, Conference Report to Accompany H.R. 4546, November 12, 2002a, Title X, p. 683.

U.S. Congress, 107th Congress, Bob Stump National Defense Authorization Act for Fiscal Year 2003, PL 107-314, Section 805, National Defense Authorization Act for Fiscal Year 2003, Washington, D.C., December 2, 2002b.

U.S. Congress, 108th Congress (1st Session—2003), National Defense Authorization Act for Fiscal Year 2004, Public Law 108-136, Washington, D.C., November 7, 2003. Online at http://www.house.gov/hasc/billsandreports/108thcongress/H1588_CR.pdf (as of December 8, 2003).